Take Action

Building a Business with the Right Mindset and Foundation

David Adam Kurz

Take Action

Printed by:
CreateSpace Independent Publishing Platform

Published in the United States of America

ISBN-13: 978-1973814313
ISBN-10: 1973814315

Here's What's Inside...

Acknowledgements

First and foremost, I need to thank my family. Notably, my mother, who has always been my is by far my biggest fan and spent her entire life trying to ensure that I was facing the right direction. Thanks go out to my brother Manny, who is a great friend and is as big a fan of me as I am his; I love telling him the things that I'm doing or involved in because he gets me! Huge fan. I love telling him the things that I am doing because he gets me! And I love hearing about his successes! I would also like to thank my beautiful, loving and supportive fiancé, Jennyffer. Her everyday support and accomplishments push me to higher limits, and help me want to succeed more and more every day. Thanks to my daughters Olivia (Pumpkin) and Amber (Boo Boo), who have always pushed me and congratulated me through every moment of weakness and triumph. Nothing in this world is as rewarding as hearing your daughters tell you how awesome you are, even when you do not see it for yourself. My step-daughters Elizabeth (Sunshine) and Allison (Sunset) are the rays of sunshine I get every time I step into my house. No matter how long a day has been, or how long I have been gone, they greet me with the most amazing energy and love. For that, they are forever in my heart.

A **huge,** special thank-you goes out to my business partner, Eric Morales and his wife Ariana—for their belief in me. It is one thing to believe in yourself, but it's a whole other deal when a close friend jumps at the chance to invest in you. I will forever thank you for the support, and look forward to the successes we will see together and to the growth of future businesses that we are already discussing.

Some folks deserve notable recognition due to their high levels of support. In business, you have to surround yourself with people who are working at high levels of success so you can mutually benefit in a constantly supportive way during this growth process. Joel "Platano" Prenza, with The 5th Color Designs in Miami, has been doing my graphic and print designs for close to a decade; I give him lots of credit toward the brand that we have developed. We did it together, brother! To Rudy Hernandez with Nu World Title and his team, thanks for your ongoing support for our agents and our company. Raul Vincent Lopez and his team, our go-to lenders, thanks for your support at high levels, such as taking calls at all hours, ensuring his team closes our deals, and supporting our clients at extraordinary levels.

Finally, to our Kurz Real Estate Agents—without your loyalty, none of this would be possible. As I have always told you, I will give you 110% of myself to you long as you give 110% to yourself as well!! My goal has always been for you to grow your business and flourish like no other entrepreneurs in this business. Together, Kurz Real Estate will remain the fastest-growing real estate company in South Florida with our eyes on the nation!

"Imagine for a moment you can build a business without all the BullShit in-between: coming up with the idea and executing the idea.
TAKE ACTION!"
– David Kurz

Introduction

Take Action!

I build my coaching around the idea that I want to help people become better entrepreneurs. I want to help them become successful. By that, I mean once somebody makes the decision to be an entrepreneur, that's what they are. Once somebody decides to sell something or go into business for themselves, they become entrepreneurs. When somebody makes the conscious decision to become a real estate agent, or a mortgage professional, they are stepping into an entrepreneurial setting. It's important for them to understand that and know this is not easy work.

Many people become real estate agents and it's easy for real estate agents to become very complacent in their work and think it's a job. I'm here to tell you it's not a job. As a real estate agent, you're an independent contractor; you don't get paid unless you sell something. That is the same for any sales job, whether you're selling lollipops, bicycles, houses, or mortgages. In the position of being an entrepreneur / independent contractor / etc., if you don't sell, you don't make money. To be successful, you need to focus on TAKING ACTION in your business and moving forward at 100mph. Knowing you will be taking risks and taking leaps of faith.

Most entrepreneurs don't know how to take the proper steps to move forward and build a foundation that will forever hold their businesses upright. No matter how many mistakes you make moving forward, if you have a strong foundation, it's much easier to recover from your mistakes.

When my entrepreneur clients are coached into success, we begin by discussing four things: their mindset, a business plan, how to move forward in their business and how to get a business properly up and running. We also coach on ways to make it a continuous success while remaining profitable; at the end of the day, that's the idea. The idea is to build a strong, successful, and profitable business.

TIP: Build a business as if you intend to sell it one day. Always think about creating so much success that your business will be worth something profitable and provable.

Enjoy the book!

I'm going to discuss the four corners of the foundation in today's market conditions; I believe it will help businesses to not only maintain the business that they have, but also continue to grow their businesses. As long as you take care of each of those foundational corners, and ensure that that foundation is well maintained, you will forever be able to build on that foundation.

TIP: Remember – you can read this book a million times but if you don't TAKE ACTION on your career, you will not have a career.

I hope this book inspires you to take the proper steps in building your business or businesses to last forever! And I hope that it inspires you to work hard, because owning a business and being an entrepreneur requires nothing more than hard, dedicated and concentrated work. Being an entrepreneur is not easy, but when you TAKE ACTION on your business and dedicate yourself to it, it will be more rewarding than any career you could have chosen.

To Your Success!

David Adam Kurz

Are You Ready for Entrepreneurship?

This chapter outlines whether or not you're ready to become an entrepreneur. Many people believe that they are ready to become entrepreneurs, but most don't have the attitude or the determination to move forward as a strong entrepreneur. So what do you need? First of all, you need the right mindset; you need to be surrounded by the right people, have the right support systems in place and you need the right plan.

It's very important to put these things together and immediately understand that this project will not be easy. Things to tell yourself on the journey:

- "I'm going to have to work my butt off."
- "People will believe that I can't get it done."
- "There will be a lot of haters and naysayers. I'll have to move forward and get past that, without allowing anyone to hold onto my ankles and drag me down."

How do you know you're ready to become an entrepreneur? It's very simple: TAKE ACTION and believe that you're ready. What changes will you have to make in taking this big step toward entrepreneurship? Simple yet again. You will have to make vast changes in your life. If you're switching from a nine-to-five job into entrepreneurship, what changes will you have to make when you take this big step toward entrepreneurship? Honestly speaking, you'll love AND hate the characteristics of the process toward solid success. They may take some getting used to at first but once you understand the dynamics of the people you surround yourself with, these alterations to your routine become simple. Some people tend to pose a negative influence on our growth and others, a positive one; you have to learn to separate the two."

Understand that I'm not telling anyone to get divorced because their spouse doesn't want to support their new business. But I am saying that if your spouse completely supports what you're doing, then your business has a better chance of being successful. My mom used to constantly repeat this phrase to me: "You are who you hang with." We'll talk more about this in the next chapter, but we want people to understand that the people who you spend the most time with will show an average of your future salary. These are a few things to keep in perspective, as you move forward into becoming an entrepreneur.

TIP: Take the group of people you hang out with the most and write down their names. Then find out their salaries and average them

out. This is your income for the year. STEP UP YOUR GAME!

Now this is the big decision: how big or small of a jump should I make in becoming an entrepreneur? It's a very scary situation to suddenly *become* an entrepreneur. It's a very weird feeling to move into leaving a job that pays you weekly or bi-weekly that has a steady income, into creating something that you'll only profit from, if you're lucky, six months to a year from the day you open. With most businesses, two years after they open they start to see a profit. This process can become very frustrating, so the size of a step you should take depends on your financial stability, and the amount of risk you're willing to take. I personally believe in big risks but I know it will either equate to an even bigger failure or an astronomical success. I am willing to see what happens because I refuse to lose.

TIP: GO BIG OR GO HOME!! You have to commit to your business at extremely high levels.

I am a true believer in the idea that if there's no risk, there's no reward. When I opened up my real estate company in Miami, Florida, I opened up a 3,000-square foot office on a very busy street in a very prominent neighborhood with five agents. I remember people telling me, "Are you crazy? You don't need 3,000 square feet to launch a business. You have five people on your team. You're losing your mind." Once I understood what they were saying, I was able to wipe away all those objections, because I knew that I wanted to jump in big. I wanted to launch my company in a big way because I am one to take big risks. Two months after opening, we signed for another 3,000 square feet, so total coverage was 6,000 square feet for the business; by that time, we had around 20 agents. After eight months from the opening, we had close to 90 agents.

So I could say that yes, I went big. However, I also understood that I had to work my butt off to make sure that I got what I wanted out of it, and we're still not done. We have a 250-agent goal for this office alone. Our goal is to open up a second office by the end of the year, with a billion-dollar sales goal in real estate, so we're doing things in a very strong, methodical and effective way. We are also being extremely vocal about it. I call it LOUD. We are being LOUD about our goals and intentions as a business. I believe in the power of expression and the universe. And I need enough people talking about our goals and intentions as a company for the universe to hear us load and clear.

Do I recommend that everyone do that? No! I do recommend that you take the first step and

TAKE ACTION. I don't care how your start, just start. Start out small, in whatever form that means for you: garage, extra bedroom, and small office, sublet an office within an office, etc. I don't care where you start - you just have to start. That's a very important part of this, and your mind should be focused completely on your business. When you start a new business, other things will suffer; that's a guarantee. Family will suffer. Free time will suffer. Friends will suffer. You will often hear your friends say, "Where have you been? You're lost. You don't hang out anymore." That's okay, because you're doing something that's going to hold you steady for a long, long time.

These are some of the important things to watch out for when you're getting into entrepreneurship. Watch for comments, like your friends saying, "Hey, you don't hang out all the time." You can't allow that to affect you. Turn around to your friends and say, "I know. I've been busy. I'm putting my business together. This is what I'm doing. By the way, I'd love your support. Be one of my cheerleaders/fans. Let everybody know what I'm doing. If you know anyone looking for my services, please let them know they can give me a call, and I know you'll vouch for me, because you are my friend. Don't worry about the fact that I'm not hanging out drinking with you every other Saturday." Just be aware of some of these minor things when going into entrepreneurship.

Another important point is your finances. You have to ensure that your finances are in order and in check, that you're not exceeding the amount of money put into your business and that you're able to live and survive. Finances can make or break family. So one of the biggest questions I get from entrepreneurs in my coaching program: "Will my family and friends change with me?" The answer is, "Yes. They will change." Some will become extra supportive and be your biggest cheerleaders. Some will become resentful that you're becoming successful in a business, and that you're no longer at their level.

Often, our friends are in similar phases of our life in its current situation, but as we begin to grow and develop stronger businesses, we make new acquaintances moving forward. Over time, these business associates will often become friends. That being said, the friends that have become complacent and have settled into a comfortable way of living without the pull to grow even further, or the family in your life that assumes you are already rolling in riches, will often be quick to judge. They will often feel resentment towards you; entrepreneurs call those the 'haters'. Should you be concerned about that? I don't think so. Haters are very important in a business. I believe that if you don't have any haters in your life, then you must be doing something wrong, and you're not pushing hard enough. Haters will talk about you. It may be in negative fashion but guess what, they are talking about you! Let them talk and let them continue to BRAND you. Some people will listen to their crap and other people will wonder what you are doing and how you are doing it so well. Enjoy the free advertising! I remember having this same conversation with a friend when I opened my Real Estate company. I got some instant haters and called my friend who is a successful business owner. I told him what was happening because I was concerned and his response was gold. He said "Dude, you should be dancing on a table right now. You should be celebrating this right now. You know what this means? It means you are making noise and people are hearing you! Soon they will be listening and you will be a leader in the industry faster than you think! They will propel you into position to do so". I hung up the phone and with a sigh of relief I thought to myself, "This is awesome!" I tell you this story so that when your time comes, you feel awesome about your success!

Take Action!

Right now, my entire coaching campaign is based on taking action (i.e. absolutely taking the step to move forward and become an entrepreneur), so if you look for #TakeAction, you'll often find pictures of me with other entrepreneurs doing big things. You have to snap into a mindset that makes you take action. Let's say you decide to become a bicycle selling entrepreneur. You'll probably open up a bike shop because that's your passion. You love bicycles, and you feel like you know everything there is to know about bicycles, so now you're going to open up a bike shop.

TIP: Visit www.DavidAdamKurz.com to learn more about our TAKE ACTION coaching and campaign.

There is a point the idea of opening that bike shop and the physical action that is filled with all kinds of thought processes: hatred, negativity, and positivity. It's a huge mixture, a combination of emotions. Because of that process someone may come along and tell you that it's not a good idea, and then the possibility arises that you might not open up the bike shop. They might show you numbers on the amount of bike shops that fail, because they open up at this time of the year, or on days and in certain markets, or whatever the case may be.

It happens with real estate companies. When I opened up my company, someone that I respected told me that (a) I was out of my mind, (b) that I would be competing against big names in the industry, and (c) what was I thinking? I thought to myself, "There are enough sales out there for all of us," so I didn't allow those comments to affect me. You have to decide, at a point, to just do it, to make it happen. Nike says it. "Just do it." They say to just get out there and get the job done. With me, it's about taking action.

It was in the middle of June when a friend of mine looked over at me in a pool in Las Vegas and said, "Why don't you have your own company?" I remember that attacking me, like a shot to the soul. My soul was telling me, "That's true. Why don't you have your own company? You're a successful real estate agent. Why aren't you doing that? You have all these great ideas. Why aren't you putting them into effect?" I remember, at that point, making the decision to take action. It didn't matter what anybody in this world was going to tell me about it. That was in the middle of June. Two weeks later on July 1st, I signed the lease for those first 3,000 square feet.

On August 3rd, we were open for business. On October 1st, I was opening up another office next door by adding another 3,000 square feet. So this is about just making things happen, and having the mindset to do them.

Now, let's make this situation as minuscule as possible. If you say one day, "I'm going to wake up early each morning and go to the gym," most of us hit the snooze button when that alarm goes off at 5 a.m. This is your one opportunity, your first opportunity of the day to take action. You could take these steps in small strides, but this is your first opportunity to hear the alarm, sit up, throw your feet on the ground, go to the bathroom, wash your mouth and your face, put on some gym clothes, and walk out the door. This is your first opportunity to take action.

Now, I bring this up because this is at the very moment that you wake up. At this one part of the day, it's so early that no one will bother you. No one is there to judge whether you follow through with it or not, but your health and your personal determination will be judged on its own. So for a moment, imagine all the folks out there who keep saying, "I'm going to go to the gym tomorrow morning," and set their alarms for 5 a.m. They go to sleep, hit the snooze button until 7:30, and whoa, guess what? Now they can't go to the gym because they have to shower, get ready, drop the kids off at school, head out to the office, and go through the normal daily grind. In this sequence, your health suffers over time.

If you woke up in the morning, sat up, put your feet on the ground, brushed your teeth, washed your face, put on gym clothes, walked out to the gym, and did that three to four times a week, how much healthier would you be? How much more energy would you have? How much longer would you be alive, if you were able to do that on a daily basis? This is your first opportunity to take action in the day.

Somebody once told me, "Always say yes to everything." I said, "Are you crazy?" They said, "Say yes to everything. Say yes to everything, and take action in your life," so I said it. Somebody said, "Why don't you have your own company?" I looked at him and said, "Yes, why don't I?" And I made it happen. I think it's critically important to overcome the mindset that there's so much in between the snooze button, putting your feet on the ground, and the idea of beginning a business and starting the business.

Taking action is important, because if you don't take action in your life, then nothing will happen. How many times have you seen a startup company roll out a great idea that you had years ago? It happens to all of us. Everyone goes through it. Everyone looks at something and says, "Wow. I thought of that a couple of years ago." The difference between you and that person is that that person took action, created it, released it on the market, and sold it; now you are watching them become successful with an idea that you had two years ago. It's important for an entrepreneur to have the mindset of just doing it and taking action.

Of course, you have to train your mind to get into the mindset of taking action. This does not happen overnight, nor is it easy. Imagine for a moment that you can remove all the bullshit in between, everything in between the idea and the action of moving forward on that idea. Imagine if you were able to take all that bullshit and kick it out the door. There's an amazing video that I saw once with Will Smith who talks about skydiving in Dubai. For those of you reading this book right now, I suggest that you go to YouTube and search for Will Smith, "skydiving in Dubai". His story is amazing, but he told the story for a different idea and a different concept. As I thought of this story, I also thought, "Imagine if I could remove all of the bullshit in between."

In the story, Will Smith is in Dubai with a bunch of friends having drinks. One of his friends screams out, "We should go skydiving tomorrow morning in Dubai. We're here." All the guys start high-fiving each other. "Yeah, let's do it. We're all going to go skydiving." Then they leave the bar. Will goes back to the hotel to get some sleep. But when he puts his head on the pillow, he thinks to himself, "Holy crap. What did I get myself into? I've never been skydiving before."

The next morning, he's in the car on his way to the skydiving site where they're going to take off on the airplane. The entire time, he's thinking to himself, "OMG, what did I do? What did I commit to? I can't believe this is happening." They reach the skydiving place, and of course, get the instruction. They have to watch a video on the possibility that people could potentially die while skydiving. Then, they get on an airplane flying through the air at 36,000 feet with the door wide open.

Now, every person is thinking to himself, "I must be out of my mind." Then they each jump out of the airplane. For Will Smith, they said, "We're going to count to three, and then we're going to jump." Later he realized that often the person counting never gets to the number three, because people will reach out and grab the door, because they get scared. So they'll say, "One, two," and they'll just throw themselves out of the plane.

When I went skydiving, my instructor told me, "I'm going to ask you, 'Are you ready?' You have to say, 'Yes,' or 'No,' and No sounds a lot like Go, so we're going to go anyway." Now I didn't have a whole lot of choice, and I knew for a fact that no matter what I said, once we were up in the air, and we were shuffling to the door, we were going out that door. Now when you jump, and you skydive, there's a one-minute free fall if you're doing the highest level possible. You get this one-minute free fall that's completely out of control. It is one of the most incredible feelings in the world. Then the guy with whom you're jumping in tandem pulls open the parachute, and all of a sudden, you're in this surreal, fantastic, peaceful, quiet environment. As a matter of fact, it's so quiet that your ears ring because your ears are accustomed to hearing noise. In this situation, it's the most blissful, surreal, amazing thing you had ever done in your life.

Will Smith had a different meaning for why he was telling that story, which you can hear by playing the clip on YouTube. Imagine going from the high-fiving, "Yes, let's go do it," to closing your eyes, to opening your eyes, to seeing yourself at the edge of the door. There was no opportunity to think to yourself, "OMG, what did I just get myself into?" Imagine for a moment that there was no opportunity for you to call your spouse and say, "Honey, I'm going skydiving." Your spouse would say, "You're out of your mind. What are you thinking? You've never done this before. You'd better not die on me."

I thought to myself, "All that stuff that you went through was erroneous. All that stuff that you went through was unimportant because you had this moment of blissfulness, of enjoyment, of the surreal reality of peacefulness, of quiet like you've never experienced before. This lasts seven minutes. The entire time leading up to those seven minutes, about twelve hours before, you were freaking out. You spent 12 hours freaking out to have seven minutes of bliss. Imagine if you could remove all of those 12 hours."

Now put that into your life, into your relationships. Stop saying you're going to do something with your wife. Take action and do it. Stop talking about visiting a new country. Figure out a plan and do it. Now, let's get to business. Stop saying one day, you're going to sell something or be an entrepreneur. Just do it, and take action in your life. Take action in your business. Do what is needed and remove all the B.S., all the naysayers, all the haters—just get them out of your head, and make it happen.

Who will stop you from taking action? Who are the naysayers? There will be people in your life who will say, "You're out of your mind. You have a great job. You have a great career. You've got a retirement plan, buddy. What are you thinking, going into business for yourself, and becoming an entrepreneur? You must be out of your mind."

But you know the truth? They can't stop you from becoming an entrepreneur. They can't prevent you from taking action. As a matter of fact, no one can. The only person that will be held responsible for that failure is you.

You are the only one who can stop yourself from taking action. Only you will prevent yourself from becoming a successful entrepreneur, not anyone else around you. Everyone else is designed to beat you up and tell you how you cannot make it happen. Now you have two options; you can curl into a corner and cry and not do anything, or you can jump up, put your feet on the ground, and TAKE ACTION.

Surround Yourself with Greatness

As a kid, my mom used to tell me, "You are who you hang with." To this day, I strongly believe that, though when you're a kid it's a bit different. If you hang with the bad kids, people assume that you're also one of the bad kids. If you hang out with the good kids, people assume you're one of the good kids. If you hang out with the smart kids, people think that you're one of the smarter kids. So if something happens, it's not just your friends who go through the consequence, it's also you, because it is assumed that you're a part of what they're doing.

As an adult and entrepreneur, it's a whole lot different. Now you have to consider the people you associate with ; you have to force yourself to be surrounded by greatness. Are they enhancing your life, your business, or your career? Are they keeping you average, or worse, are they dragging you down? You need to ask these questions when you think about the people in your life.. It's very difficult to step away from the group of friends that you've been friends with forever. Note that I'm not saying you *can't* be friends with them anymore. I'm just saying you have to be decisive on who you're spending your time with.

You need to choose to spend your time with **Key People**. Key People are those that enhance your life by pushing you toward internal growth. They should be above or ahead of you in some way. If you're the top of the food chain in your group, then there's no one to learn from. Go somewhere and be around people who you can consistently learn from. One of the things that we've decided to do at our company, Kurz Real Estate, is to create an open and collaborative environment very similar to something you would see at a company like Google or Apple; companies that require people to interact and be creative amongst each other. We did that with the idea of people surrounding themselves with greatness in the form like-minded individuals. We hire great agents and surround them with talented agents who can help them develop their skills. They feed off of each other, pushing themselves into the next level in their careers. We understood that principle, and believe it or not, the results are amazing.

Surround yourself with amazing business partners, even people who are in your same exact business, your competitors. Become friendly with them. Learn from them, and then you will become much stronger.

Think about the concept of '*birds of a feather flock together*', of being the people that you hang out with the most. That is who you are. Take those people, average out their salaries, and that will be your income. Your education level will remain the same. Your income and lifestyle will remain the same. If you want to break out of your income, break out of your way of life. Know more and learn more, then upgrade your surrounding group.

People ask me about this: "Well, I have friends, and they've been my friends for a very long time." You can remain friends with them. Just ask yourself this question: how much time do you spend on them? What are the chances of you making somebody better? People say, "David, what if I'm able to enhance myself, and then enhance the other ones around me?" You can't change people or force them to be like you, and you can't force them to make changes for the better. You can't force them not to want to be where they are. Some people are perfectly happy at their nine-to-five job, and living (what I consider to be) their average life.

For a moment, you may think, "How is that possible?" That's what they're happy with; it's their idea of success. That is their idea of progression. They've got the white picket fence, the two-car garage, the nine-to-five, the beautiful spouse, and two children, like "cookie-cutter" American families. You can't become an entrepreneur and force that person to become an entrepreneur with you. It's basically impossible. You can try to make it happen but you can't make the "horses drink the water". You can say, "Why don't you do this since you're interested in that?" They may say, "Wow. What a great idea," but then they don't do what we just talked about: TAKE ACTION. Now, you're in a position where you can't grow, because you keep surrounding yourself with people like that.

Does this apply to your friends? Can it also be applied to your spouse and family? Absolutely but unfortunately, you will have to cut out some family members a little bit. You will have to see them at Christmas, New Year's, or Hanukkah, whatever you decided to do with your family, friends, and spouse. Your spouse is one of the biggest influencers. You need to find a way to get your spouse on board with whatever it is that you're going to be doing. Get them to support what you're going to be doing because this is the person you wake up to, and come home to, every single day. This is the person who you close your eyes and go to sleep with every single day.

If your spouse is not on board, it's tough for you to do what you're doing. You will spend an enormous amount of time working hard on your business and they will not understand it because they have zero interest; they're not involved. In the very least, all you need is their 110% support. "Great job; I don't know what you're doing, but go get it done," or "Hey, I'm more interested in learning about what you're doing. Is there any way I can help you?" That would be astronomically better.

Once you accept that you cannot change people, then you will have to figure out:

- How much time you spend with them
- How much time you need to be around them.
- Who you should be spending your time around.

How do you find the positive people who will enhance your life, your career, or your business? Networking events and local business groups are a start: there are plenty of great groups out there, including BNI (Business Network International). Try sports and entertainment groups or self-development groups. Invest in yourself by hanging around the people you want to be around.

Once you start making a little money, go to places where they hang out, the people that you want to learn from. If you're thinking of attracting at really high levels, those places can be pricey. Someone told me a story about how he would hang out in the ritzy parts of Manhattan so that he could surround himself with the right crowd, and learn from the right crowd; keep in mind he didn't have a pot to piss in. He would order club soda "on the rocks" in a glass, and hang out by pretending to have a drink with everybody. All he did was sip club soda all night long, so the bill came out to whatever club soda costs, but it wasn't $25 a drink. But he was surrounded by the right people, and he took those necessary steps. Now that particular person is a widely successful real estate agent in Manhattan, and trust me—there's no more club soda in his cup. He's doing much better now.

Networking—that's how you can make sure to surround yourself with and find the right people. Networking is a huge thing. You just have to go to the right places, meet the right people. Follow up with those people, and be relentless in being around them.

Be Relentless

Being **RELENTLESS** means ensuring that you are relentless about the success of your company; you're relentless about generating new business, maintaining the business that you have, and relentless in your follow-up when it comes to new and previous clients. It's important to be relentless at all these different levels. Focus— take all of your energy and be uncompromising about what makes you money. These are called money-making tasks.

If that means that you have to send note cards and make phone calls, you must have a proper client-relationship management tool in place to remind you on the timing of a call to a customer, their birthday, and their kid's birthdays. Imagine if you got a call when it was your son or your daughter's birthday from the guy who sold you a car and said, "Hey, I just wanted to call you and wish your son/ daughter a happy birthday." How would that make a difference in your relationship with that car salesman? It would be huge!

When we talk about being relentless in my coaching, we have a philosophy on follow-up. We say that you follow up with somebody until they either say "Yes," (which requires a different follow-up), they die, or they get a restraining order. If they get a restraining order, find a way to refer the business to someone else in your industry and get a referral fee for that business. If they die, find out if there is a probate issue you can help with! The idea here is to be relentless in your business at all different levels, and become a nonstop machine. This will be the winning formula that will help you grow your business.

Have Self-Discipline

An old proverb says, "If it were easy, everyone would do it." You have to build a business on the discipline that is required by every entrepreneur who needs to grow a business. Entrepreneurs have to develop a very specific self-discipline. They have to be disciplined in their business and in their lives.

A MUST KNOW: An entrepreneur needs to understand that waking up early is important, going to sleep late will probably happen, and everything in-between will be focused on becoming an influential business owner and a strong entrepreneur.

You develop self-discipline by putting plans into effect. You have to put a plan into effect to ensure the outcome of your entire day; you have to work hard at being specific on your daily tasks. You do all the things necessary to grow your business and enhance your life. Put this plan together, and then practice, practice, practice. Practice your plan until it becomes a habit.

Once it becomes habitual, that is the discipline that you have created within yourself. You wake up early, go to the gym, get to the office, make follow-up phone calls and visits, send note cards, visit old clients, do drop-offs, and meet new clients. Everyone I've met goes into my system.

Every email is documented. Maybe, at some point, I get to sleep. If you can create a system that describes every single day of your life, those days will become habitual. It's funny how twenty years after their service has ended, after having been in the military for twenty years, their eyes open automatically at 5am. It becomes habitual for that person. The words they say, the mannerisms they have, and the things they do are based on the discipline that they learned while in the military.

You can teach yourself to be that way too. If you need to, go crazy and hire a coach who will help you put this discipline into effect. Again, the coach can only guide you, give you a schedule, and teach you how to follow it. You have to TAKE ACTION in your discipline to ensure that you're taking the steps necessary to become habitual in what you're doing for yourself. Yes, coaches cost money. But is enhancing your career worth it? Someone once told me that their coach was $1,000 a month. $12,000 a year! What if this investment yielded you another $100,000 a year in income? Now would the $12,000 be worth the investment in YOURSELF?

Sweat the Small Stuff

We always hear this saying, "Don't sweat the small stuff." I'm here to tell you that this is probably the worst advice you could ever receive. When you're creating a business for yourself, all the small stuff is critical. All of the minor details matter. If you start to think to yourself, "Don't sweat the small stuff," then the small stuff will grow. They'll add up and up and up, until they become the big stuff businesses fail because of.

There are stories about how basketball superstar, Michael Jordan was "sweating the small stuff", down to the point that he would match his car to the suit that he was wearing that day. When I heard that story, I thought to myself, "Think about the discipline of Michael Jordan putting his hand on a basketball. Think about how he would reflect on the importance of his fingertips' on the basketball, how he sweated the small stuff when it came to very specific items. Maybe that's why he's still the greatest basketball player that anyone's ever known."

It's so important to think about these things and attack them as soon as they come to light. A small thing happens; address it. A little thing happens; address it so these small things don't become the big thing that you're now spending all this time and energy on attacking and trying to make it all small again. Small things are easier to control in your business. Once something has gotten to the point of being a big problem, then it becomes a colossal, overwhelming issue. It takes a lot of energy and a lot of time for you to solve, so solve these things very early on or they will consume you immensely.

Focus on the End Result

When you put together your business plan, concentrate on the end result. What is the result you are looking for or looking to accomplish? Please don't focus on the cash because your income and commissions, the money that you make, will be a consequence of how you conduct your business. If you do your business badly and unethically, you won't make money as a consequence, but if you conduct your business in an efficient and positive manner, then you will receive money as the consequence. Find out what you want as a result and act on it.

Some people will call it your 'why.' Why are you doing this? Once you know your result, you can plan for it accordingly. When someone sits with me and says, "This is the end goal, the result of what I want to do in the next 12 months," I say, "Great. I'm so glad that you brought that up, because we always start with the end result in mind, and then we work our way backward." You see, if you have the end result, you can now decide what you will do for the year. Break that down into quarters, then into months, and then into weeks; break that down into tangible and manageable dates. If you're able to follow your daily plan for 365 days, there's an excellent possibility that you will reach your end result, goal and income desired.

The Four Corners to the Foundation

The next few chapters will show the four corners of the foundation in today's business the way I see them and they way you should see them moving forward. We're going to talk about how to implement and take care of each corner so that your foundation remains strong. The four corners of the foundation that I will bring to light are: your database, your social media, your website and web presence, and your print media.

We will review all four corners so you can focus on these four topics in your business today and forever, moving forward. Now, keep in mind that social media is still a new thing. Ten years ago, the foundation was a bit different. Also keep in mind that in ten years from now, the foundation may adjust a little bit, you'll have to make those adjustments. You will have to figure out how to maintain your foundation as you move forward and the world changes; you will have to change with it. For the folks who are still living in the world of a decade ago, and neglecting social media, they will in no way grow their businesses at the level you can if you focus on yours. Especially at the speed and effectiveness you can have by properly adapting to the foundation of today.

Does a foundation work for both small businesses and large firms? Of course!! Regardless of your type of business, everyone must have: a database, a strong social media presence, a website, a web presence, and print campaigns. Small companies can do this at a smaller level. Larger corporations (i.e. Coca-Cola, Proctor & Gamble, McDonald's, Burger King) do it at a very high level. They have proper databases and an established social media presence; they know how to go after the right people. They have a High-speed, and optimized website, and a dominating web presence with web ads, and print articles in magazines and flyers. Each company has everything you can think of to stay in your face consistently.

As your company continues to grow, remember to properly maintain each one of these. As you grow and become busier, you can potentially neglect one of the four corners. Guaranteed, if you neglect one of the four corners, then your foundation will get cracked, get forgotten, or crumble. Now your business will be at risk of failing somewhere because you didn't take care of your foundation appropriately. As you grow in your business, I advise that your very first hire in any business is an assistant. Your assistant can now focus on maintaining a lot of your foundation, doing all of the required nitty-gritty work to ensure that your foundation stays intact.

As you grow and become busier, you may not have as much time to maintain your foundation, but it doesn't make it any less important. In fact it's becoming more important as your business is growing, and you'll have to focus some thought on this foundation through hiring the best people to help and assist you in maintaining it.

Database

The first and most important part of your foundation is your database. If you don't have anyone to sell to, then you can't sell anything. Many people do not even pay real attention to this. They sell here and there and don't really put forth attack tactics toward a database! Your database is so very important. The easiest way to initially build your database is through your telephone. In this day and age, everyone has a smartphone with names, email addresses, and phone numbers. That is your first and most immediate database. That is the database in your life that will initially begin your business. If you look through your phone and you only have phone numbers, then it's time to reach out to those people in your phone and get those email addresses. Have multiple avenues of approach and communication.

Most real estate professionals will initially sell a house to a family member or a friend. I believe that is the same for just about any business. If you're selling computers, chances are you will reach out to your family and friends and ask them who needs a computer. It's the same with bicycles or roller skates. If you've become a stylist at a salon, and you're paying for that chair, you will want to do someone's hair. The first people you reach out to will be your family and friends, and hope that they trust you to cut their hair.

Some other places that you can look to build your database are some of the other events discussed earlier: networking events, business events, business groups, development groups, self-development groups, coaching programs, and social media. You can do so many different things to build a proper database. Clients will ask me, "Should I purchase email lists?" My response is, "No," because when you buy an email list, no one knows who you are- you need to create a name and brand for yourself before you begin to gather emails.. Maybe it would help with exposure but you can get that off social media.

If you were able to ensure that people knew who you were, and you could find a way to appropriately build your database through your social media platform or web presence, where people volunteer their information, then you are on the right track. It's important to reach out to your family and friends, asking them to share with you their sphere of influence. This is another way of building your database.

When you go to networking events, you're receiving business cards and speaking to people who can bring you their business. You're getting to know who they are, telling them who you are, and you're figuring out ways of working together so you can enhance your business. Most people will go home and throw that business card on the desk and forget about it, but that business card needs to go into your database immediately. You need to have an email system and a way to track your database.

I use an email system to send out blast emails, and a client relationship management (CRM) tool that allows me to keep track of both my current clients, and the point of the sale they're in. It is very important that I keep track of those people not in my CRM tool because this means they are prospective clients or future clients. Those folks are sitting inside of my email blast system.

There are a few email management companies that you can review, from Contactually to Constant Contact to MailChimp. I prefer Constant Contact, but MailChimp is free up to 2,000 people. You have to decide what you want to do, and how you can grow your business that way. At networking events, when you receive those business cards, you take that contact information (name, email address, phone number) and enter it right into your email database. That way, you're emailing folks on a consistent basis; you're staying in front of their faces. When you meet somebody, don't be afraid to send them a video.

Walk away, grab their business card, put the information on your phone, and send them a quick *selfie video* thanking them for the opportunity to have met them. They'll never forget you - I promise that.

STAY IN EVERYONES FACE ALL THE TIME!

Now that you have this database of people saved inside of your email management system, and all of the clients in your CRM, now you need to utilize and maintain it. I believe in emailing people at least once or twice a day. Many people would say that's crazy; that you shouldn't email that much, but let me explain something about emails. When you receive something you consider junk, it's only junk email because you're not interested in purchasing what you may need at that very moment, or what they're selling at that very moment. That's why it's considered junk email. If you needed what they were selling, then it wouldn't be junk email.

However, very few of us will go into the email, scroll all the way to the bottom, and click the unsubscribe button—which will open another page that will ask us if we're sure we want to unsubscribe. We will say, "Yes." That will open another section that says, "Why do you want to unsubscribe?" Very few people will do that; it's much easier just to highlight or check off your email, and delete it. However, if you're emailing them every single day, no matter what happens when they receive your email – whether they delete or open it does not matter – they see your name every single day: David Adam Kurz, Professional Coach, Real Estate Broker.

When they do need something from you, and they do see that email – which is just a matter of time – they will open your email and see how they can contact you. Maybe someday they will say to a friend who is thinking of buying a home, "Man, this guy emails me all the time. Next time I get his email, I'm going to let you know." Now they're referring you to somebody because you've been in their face consistently.

TIP: STAY IN EVERYONES FACE ALL THE TIME!

You have to maintain this database; make sure you're constantly adding people into this database. You can even categorize the kinds of people you have. For instance, I have a list of realtors and I have a list of previous clients and a list of current clients. I have a list of out-of-country contacts, then I break those down into Venezuela, Israel, New York City, etc. I break it down to specific groups because not every email is meant for everybody. If I'm announcing a local event, I may not send that to contacts in Israel. However, if I'm announcing a property that I'm selling, or if I'm announcing a new agent on my team, that might go to everyone.

That's information I want everyone to know. Regardless of where they are and who they are. This is information telling my contacts that we are busy, growing and capable of handling any business they put in our path.

The other thing you must look into is the creation of a "drip campaign", because anything you can do to automate your life would make it so much better. Automation is a key tool for a professional in sales. The more you can automate, the easier your life and business will be. All these email systems have a way for you to create the email, and then set a day and time for it to be sent out. It doesn't need to be sent immediately, so you could spend an hour creating ten emails, and have them set up for the next dates without a problem. You can create 30, 40, or 50 emails; when you drop somebody's name in there, they will automatically get these emails in the way that you've set it up.

I recommend drip campaigns for people who are currently interested in what you're trying to sell. So if you put out a Facebook ad campaign that talks about the product you're selling (bicycles, real estate, etc.), and somebody registers because of that, it could mean potential interest in what you're selling. If that falls into a great drip campaign that consistently drips emails about the new product that you have, or something that's going on in your business (i.e.

check out this new style of house, check out this new bicycle with these cool tires), you're staying in their face in an automated way. This doesn't mean you don't call and attempt contact. But this will ensure you remain in front of them consistently.

Every name falls in that database. You don't have to do it over and over again as you will end up creating systems that are automated, that free up your time, but stay in people's faces for you. You have to be everywhere all the time!

Who goes into your database? Every single person that you know. Even you grandparents!

Social media communication is important. Who is on social media? Probably every single person you can imagine. Your grandmother will forget what you do for business if you don't stay in her face and remind her. It's the honest truth. People forget what you do because they just don't care about your life, they care about their own. You have to consistently remind them of what you're doing for a living, especially your friends who are accustomed to hanging out with you for a few drinks once in a while. If you remind them consistently about your business, they will remember you when the time comes, whether it's for them or someone they know outside of your network. This will allow you to build your database consistently.

When you're on social media, keep in mind that social media communication is important and to send private messages to people. Answer people back. Listen to what people are doing, and then comment on it.

Social Media

Social media is the second part of the foundation we want to discuss. A social media following, in today's day and age, is probably the most important aspect of building your database. This tool would allow you the opportunity to build a stronger database beyond people whose contact info you may not have, but you've connected with them through social media.

Building a strong following is important. Sometimes I will meet people on the street and have a conversation with them, and they will say to me, "Oh, you're David Kurz. I follow you on social media." Having communicated with them previously on social media, it's almost as if we know each other already. We walk out to each other saying, "Hey, what's going on? I know you. You know me," though we've never physically met before. Having that physical meeting after being connected for so long on social media, there is euphoria to that acknowledgment.

Having a strong social media presence is important. In another example, I recently sold my car and began depending solely on Uber for rides. (Holy crap this was hard to do!) I found that riding Uber does two things for me. Number one, it saves me a ton of money. Number two, it allows me to have more productivity time doing some money-making tasks mentioned earlier.

Instead of driving through Miami traffic without checking my phone, email or social media, I can sit in the back of the Uber to work and focus on the things that are productive for my business. Now, sitting in traffic for an hour is not as detrimental to my business as it used to be. I can't even begin to tell you how much time I have lost sitting in traffic. Now, I sit in the car and work while someone who gets paid to sit in traffic does just that.

The other day I had an Uber gentleman pick me up. Now, I'm very big on branding. Branding is probably the one thing that is extremely important for your business. You want recognition, so when we talk about branding, I speak of everything down to your social media profile photo. My profile photo is the same photo that I use for my Uber profile and marketing. It's the same photo that I use for just about any profile: LinkedIn, YouTube, and Instagram.

Because I do that, the first thing that my Uber driver said when he picked me up was, "Hey, man. You're David Kurz, Kurz Real Estate." I said, "Yes, I am." He says, "I follow you on social media. A picture came up, and I had to pick you up."

I thought that that was so impressive. That was the first time it had ever happened to me. I had met people before who had seen me or had followed me on social media, but never a follower who I had never connected with in any way. An Uber driver who decided, "I have to pick up this person because I follow them as an influencer on social media." That was huge for me.

The next time that happened was at the dry cleaners. I pulled up to the dry cleaners. (I got rid of my car, but I do have a toy: a Slingshot.) A Slingshot is a three-wheeled vehicle; it has two wheels in the front, and one in the back; it's a very cool ride, but with no doors and wide open. I use the Slingshot every once in a while. Recently I had two months of dry cleaning that I had been lollygagging on and never got dropped to the cleaners. Since I had not been to the dry cleaners in a few months, I did not know that they had closed down.

I said, "I'm going to drop off this bag at the cleaners on my way to the gym." I get to the cleaners with this huge bag of clothes on the passenger seat, and the cleaners are closed for the next six to nine months for construction. Since I'm in the Slingshot, I can't say, "Okay, fine, let me throw this in the trunk, and I'll go to the gym," because there is no trunk.

A gentleman in a dry cleaners truck, from another locally known business, pulls to the side and says, "Hey, buddy, you need help?"

I thought, "This guy is a genius. He's hanging out at a closed cleaner's facility looking for business." I said, "Absolutely, I need help." He says, "Great," and pulls over to the side. I liked his hustle; I liked his grind. Instantly I said, "You've earned my business." I filled out the form, I gave him my clothes, and he took off.

The owner of the store where the clothes went, called me to say, "Mr. Kurz, I just want to thank you for working with so-and-so, who is the driver." I said, "Listen, your driver has an amazing hustle. I appreciate what he's doing to earn business, and I felt the need to give him my business." He said, "Well, I just want you to know that we saw your name, and we all follow you on social media. We appreciate your influence on us, and we appreciate what you're teaching us about sales and aggression." I thought to myself, "Holy crap, did this really just happen?"

I'm not saying that your level of social media needs to be at *that* level (or maybe it does). No matter what you're selling, you have to be the influencer of what you're selling. At a low or a high level, depending on what you want to be and what you want to do, you need to be pushing on a social media platform at very high levels, utilizing great photos and video to the maximum.

Push YouTube and Facebook videos, boost those relevant posts that need to get in front of people's faces, do targeted ads, and ensure that your business is staying in front of people's faces so that they use you. Targeted Ads are much more effective than boosting so do your research. Learn it or even better – hire someone who knows what they are doing to handle it for you.

Having heard these stories, do you think, when the time came to buy a new home, that the Uber Driver and dry cleaning owner would not call me? Of course they will call me, because I'm so consistently in their faces that both guys saw an application for service (whether it was the Uber app or the application for cleaning services) with my name on it and they recognized it. It didn't have a picture or any other feature, it just had my name (David Adam Kurz) and it pushed out. When people go to my Facebook profile, which is **@DavidAdamKurz**, they will like it, and they will follow me. I will often put out tidbits on sales techniques; I share a little bit about my life, but I focus on taking action, sales, and real estate.

Now, there are two key parts to my business. My main business is running a real estate brokerage. My other business is coaching and building entrepreneurs and investment training. This means that I need to be in so many people's faces at very high levels of exposure. If I'm not, then

I'm not doing my agents any good because my agents depend on me to brand our company so well and at such lengths, when they go out to meet a buyer or a seller, they know who we are.

It's so important to think about that. When my agents go out and they sit at a listing appointment or a buyer's appointment, the buyer or the seller says, "Oh, you're at Kurz Real Estate? We know David Kurz. We follow him on social media." You already have an advantage on anyone else out there. I think it's so important to become an influencer in what you're selling and becoming strong on your social media platforms.

There is a difference between a personal page and a public business page on Facebook. Often people will ask me, "Should I make my personal page public?" My answer is "Yes." If it's personal information, why in the world are you putting it on social media? Whatever you put on social media should be something you want to share with the world. Now, I built my platform utilizing my personal social media page first. I didn't have a business page right away, so my personal social media page was the platform that I used to launch everything that I was doing. I was able to build that with friends, friends of friends, family, and friends of the family.

As it was built, eventually my Facebook page got to the point where 5,000 people had "friended" me, and I was maxed out. At that point, I decided to carbon-copy my personal base and created a business page. On the business page, I keep it 100% business. In my personal page, I mix it up and keep it business and fun and pleasure: like, trips to the park, nights out at a beautiful restaurant, or a night out at a bar. Oh, by the way, I also sold this house, or one of my agents has this house for sale, so forth and so on. I keep it interesting for people to want to participate in what I'm putting out there.

I can leverage myself on social media and leverage my company; I can leverage my speaker base and leverage my clients on social media. Again, social media is one of the most important platforms that you must get accustomed with. If you're not on social media, you're seriously out of your mind. The top four social media platforms that you should be engulfed in are Facebook, Instagram, LinkedIn, and YouTube.

Mark my words: video is the future of the Internet. No one will want to read an article on how to do something anymore—now they YouTube it. Before, it used to be all about Google.

How do I change the alternator in my Ford F-150? Google it, and you would be able to find PDF instructions on how to change the alternator on your Ford F-150. People will go to YouTube to get a how-to video, because often you're reading instructions to something and getting them confused. It takes you twice as long in that process, whereas if you're watching a video on how to do it, there it is.

When you're selling houses, you have to do a video on yourself. Then do a video on the houses, and a video on the neighborhoods. Facebook launched live video, Instagram launched Instagram Live and Instagram Stories. There are so many different ways to put yourself out there through social media platforms. It's very important that you focus on your social media and build your business. However, social media is not a replacement for your website.

Website and Web Presence

Your website is the third part of your foundation. Your website and your web presence are just as important as your social media presence. The difference between the two is that social media requires your interaction at least 8 to 10 times a day, whereas your website is the window to who you are.

A website is important because people will Google you to do business with you. Even if they've met you and want to do business with you, there is a little voice in the back of their head that says, "Research this person and learn more about them." They will go to their smartphone or computer, and do a Google search on your name. I have seen agents lose business because they do not have a website. A client they are working with decides to research them and finds nothing. This is the big red flag of "HEY! I'm a new agent". And although you can spin this into "No one will work harder for you", some clients may not want to be your guinea pig. Clients need to know you have a presence and they need to know you have the know-how to get the job done.

In my case, they will search 'David Adam Kurz' to find the kind of presence you have online. Now my presence online is important. I have public relations in check. I have social media in check.

I have websites in check, so when I am Googled, I take up a good portion of the first and/or second page of the search results; I have enough content on the web to validate what I do. I also have videos on YouTube, etc. Google owns YouTube, so when you Google my name, many of my YouTube videos will appear.

It's important to have a website as a window to who you are, a connection to what you sell, and a connection to your social media platforms; it should be maintained always and consistently with your business. Building a website for yourself is important. If you're in the sales business, you should never leverage your company to build a website for you. For example, if you join a nationally known real estate company, there's a very big chance that they will offer you a free website. You don't own this and as an entrepreneur you should own your own media and marketing.

When I first launched my brokerage a broker friend of mine told me, "Make sure you offer enough stuff to make it painful for them to leave." I thought to myself, "What does that even mean?" He said, "If you offer a free CRM and a free website, and free this and free that, when they think about leaving, there will be a pain factor because they will lose all of this. They will lose their web presence." I thought to myself immediately, "Why in the world would I want to work with somebody who does not want to work with me anymore?" But I do understand what he meant to say. Web presence is so important it would be painful for an agent to lose it. So they would stay with you to avoid years of marketing that website lost forever. That is how important a web presence is!

For a lot of companies, it's a numbers game. If I can retain as many agents as possible, then I'm winning. In my opinion, it's a "quality game". How many quality professionals can I get in my company who want to work with me and within my culture? For those of you who are working with a company offering you a website, take a little time to Google some companies that will make inexpensive and fantastic websites for you. Go to companies like tigertech.net or godaddy.com who will sell you a website name for $20 for the two years that you can redirect to whatever website you purchase and use, and maintain that website.

Your website should have some key features. First of all, it should talk about who you are as an individual or a sales person. It should talk about your company and what you stand for. You should have a blog page, which will allow you the opportunity to say what's happening and what projects you're involved in or working on.

I sell real estate. My agents sell real estate, so our homes and communities are important to what we do. When we build a website, we will often blog about the neighborhoods in which we are selling. For instance, it would not be odd for a real estate agent to write a review about a restaurant on their blog. Why? That restaurant falls within the area where that real estate agent sells homes. Writing a review about a restaurant tells people that the agent really knows the area and that they're excited to be selling homes there. The agent can find you a great home in a neighborhood that also has great restaurants.

This is something that you can use no matter what business you're in. If you sell bicycles, chances are you can write blogs about different bicycles; you can blog about bike routes that people can take, biking events in your community, and so forth. This lets people know that not only do you sell bicycles, but also you fit in with the lifestyle of a true bicyclist.

Video blogs also known as VLOGS are extremely effective to your business. Notice we have spoken a lot about video in this book. We discuss it because video has truly revolutionized how we relay our messages. You can do this effectively on your blogs by posting the YouTube videos you create. In case you are lost, everything gets connected everywhere. These videos are so much easier to promote. BUT remember words on a blog, Google can pick up. I have seen instances where growing entrepreneurs have created videos, posted them on a blog on their website and then created a full description of the video. Basically everything they said on the video is narrated in writing on the blog. NOW, they have officially created a VLOG that can be promoted on YouTube and Facebook along with a written blog that would be picked up by search engines such as Google in order to help with SEO on the website.

TIP: SEO is built overtime with original content on your website. This is not an overnight success. You have to work hard on this and build it so your site gains ranking on search engines!

Those are some of the key features that you need to have on your website. Then, of course, you need to have the window to what you're selling. In my case, I need to be able to showcase homes, so my website needs to be connected to our multiple listing services (MLS services) that will allow people to search for properties on my website. Going back to the bicycle analogy, you need to showcase your inventory with an ecommerce setup so that people can purchase bicycles on your website.

There are reasons why companies like Amazon are so popular. You can go to amazon.com, search for something, buy it right on the website, and it'll be delivered to you in a couple of days. As a business owner, you should be offering such services. Even if you are local, calculate the cost of shipping, figure out how to build a good eCommerce setup, and ensure the platform where your eCommerce is set up is capable. Make sure that the credit card purchases you're receiving online are real, and that you're not shipping bicycles to people with stolen credit cards. (I am coming from experience here.) I once owned a motorcycle shop in the heart of Miami. We had official bike nights and everything having to do with selling motorcycles and accessories. I set up an online shop and received some really great orders for helmets and parts only to find out that the cards were stolen and the money would be pulled right back out of the company account. It was a huge blow to me and the company and an incredible lesson learned. FAIL FORWARD or read this and learn this here so you don't have to fail and can allow my failure to help guide you.

Make sure that you know what you're doing. You could hire somebody to teach you what to do, or do the appropriate research like any person has the right to do. Go to Google and learn the good, the bad and the ugly of having an online eCommerce store. Remember that if you're selling something, this Is the easiest way to sell without someone physically coming to a store and purchasing a product. It opens up your business to the world!! It is the difference of having a local bike shop and a national brand and business that can be easily found and accessible. One you can work with immediately. Why in the world do you think AMAZON is so damn successful.

That is the last real deal feature you need to have. Of course, you will have a 'contact' section where people should contact you; in my case, I enjoy having a forced registration. Some folks are very afraid to include a forced registration because they feel that if you're forced to register, people will not stay on your website and they'll find another place. That's okay, you know why? The people who do register are serious about purchasing your product. You have to consider that they're already enjoying your website, which means they want to be there and they want to potentially work with you. So they register.

It limits the number of fakes in your profile database for your clientele; it gives you people who are more serious about making a purchase with you directly.

TIP: You should hire somebody to build your website. I have seen people who will try to

<u>build their websites with these easy, do-it-yourself deals, and they're never very good websites. They don't understand the structure of a website for they business they are in.</u>

Remember, whatever you do for a living, that's what you do. I sell houses. I'm not a web designer. I know how to sell houses. I know how to coach entrepreneurs. I know how to speak in front of people and motivate a crowd, and I know the business. I do not know how to build a website and I have zero interest in it. So naturally, I want to hire somebody who builds websites all day long and has zero interest in selling houses.

I hope that this makes sense to you because it boils down to the point of hiring the right person to do the right job. When you're looking for somebody to hire to build your website, make sure that you won't get ripped off because websites are fairly affordable. Often companies have already built a website similar to the one that you want, and they can show it to you. If those two things are in effect, then you have a good situation.

In real estate, many companies give you platforms, layouts, and websites that are so easy to purchase at good prices with minimal maintenance fees on a monthly basis.

I'm sure that this exists for just about every single business; you should look into them and do the appropriate research to get a website that fits your style and your needs.

You should have creative rights, but allow the web designers to tell you about customer-friendly websites, how the websites behave and react. Don't try to become a website designer because that is not what you do for a living. Allow somebody who does that to focus on what will make your website more user-friendly, so the customer remains on your website for as long as possible.

Your website should be posted and exposed in every place possible. Remember what I said at the beginning of this chapter, your social media links should be accessible on your website so that people can connect to you through your social media. In your social media, your website should be posted so people can connect to your website. In your social media, you're building a following. People will love what you're doing, but when they're finally serious about buying whatever you're selling, they will click on your website, utilize your eCommerce store, and make purchases through there. What you are trying to do is ensure that you cross-reference every avenue of communication and exposure.

Your database, which we spoke about a few chapters ago, should be receiving consistent emails from you. Every single email should have a link to all of your social media platforms and a link to your website. Every single email that you send should have a link to your website. You can build a stronger web presence through your blog and through participating on other websites. Writing blogs and articles for other, similar, websites that have to do with your field of expertise, is great exposure. This exposure can translate to people hearing about you and your website much more and to a slightly different audience than you'd normally have.

If you're in a business that requires extreme exposure, look into public relations (PR). Spend some money with a PR person who can give you proper web exposure. This is not just about having a website, it's about having web exposure. You have a website and it'll be fully dedicated to your business. You'll be able to push a lot of information through there.

Through your YouTube channel, you'll be pushing a lot of videos; this will be the future of the Internet. . Do all the research that you want. You will find that just about everyone is turning to video versus articles. They want to see the news, not read the news, and it's becoming a bigger every day.

You need to be making videos, posting them on YouTube, and creating that web presence so when somebody Google's your name, not only does your website appear, but your videos and social media do as well. Hopefully you've been writing for other places, and their sites come up. If you can dominate a page of Google, I promise that you will have the necessary web presence to give you the certification into work with an end user or a client.

Print

The fourth corner of the foundation of your business is print. Now I know some of you are thinking right now, "How is that even relevant today? You just spent all this time telling me to have an online database, social media, a website, and a web presence." However, print in today's day and age is still very important because it solidifies your branding aspect.

Print continues to help brand you. Think about this for a minute. Did Versace stop taking out articles in fashion magazines just because there was an online platform? Did McDonald's stop taking out ads in magazines because they have a website? Of course this is not the case. Now I'm not telling you to go out and spend tons of money on ads. As a matter of fact, I'm a bit anti-print ad.

However, that is not the only print method. Print means quality business cards, posters, and fliers that you can place in different locations. Print includes tablecloths with your logo on it, so when you do presentations, you have a setup. All of these tools are print, so let's talk about some of the main print features.

I want you to think about having brochures for the products that you sell. Those brochures should be in a PDF version on your website as well as a print version that somebody can touch and hold when they come to your location. If somebody comes to my real estate office to ask about a project being developed in the local area, I've made it a point to grab brochures from each of those projects so that they can physically hold and look at a book on the project. I can follow up that meeting with an email, showing them all the information that they need on a website platform for a purchase of the home in that new development.

If you're selling bicycles or lollipops or burgers, it doesn't matter. You need to have something people can hold and look at. There is a reason why restaurants still have menus, rather than a digital version of it on an iPad. There are some cool restaurants that are trendy, and they have iPads stuck inside the table, and that's how you can order your food.

People didn't rush to replace menus with iPads because it removed the personal aspect of it. It took away the feel of the menu, looking up at a waiter or a server, and asking that server, "What's the best thing on the menu" to get a true opinion, and having that person write it down on a pad so they could later go punch it into a computer. Brochures are an excellent way to display your products.

However, I will tell you this about every single print item moving forward. Ensure it is of quality. If it is not a quality product, do not waste your time. Now I understand that some of you reading this book may not have the money to spend on strong, hard, quality paper but you will have to start somewhere. I get it, but the second that you're able to reinvest in yourself and improve the quality of your handouts to people, do so.

Do not slip up on this because the quality of the brochure and the way it feels in someone's hands says a lot about the way you promote your business, how you handle your business, and the quality of your product. You could have the most quality product in the world but if you present it in a sorry, nasty way, no one will purchase your product. However, if you have a great quality product and it is a quality presentation, you will win consistently.

Let's talk about 'every day direct mail' for a moment (EDDM). The United States Post Office offers this service that gives a seller or a company the ability to create postcards and mail delivery professionals leave them in everybody's mailbox on certain routes you've chosen online. Now, many agents in my business have built their businesses utilizing EDDM. I'm not against it. As a matter of fact, I think that it's a complement to your business.

I do not believe that EDDM is the way to obtain business today. I believe that it is a *complement* to your branding to remind people who you are. I believe that if you can stay in their email box and in their face through targeted ads on Facebook and social media, you're already ahead of the game. Once you start making enough money, you can utilize EDDM to be the cherry on top of your social media web presence platforms.

Once people have been bombarded with your face and your product for so long, they'll notice your stuff in the mailbox. You and I know when you pull out the mail and you go through every piece of laminated card stock paper, you just throw it in the trash. Very rarely do you look at it. You need brand recognition so your brand must be in their face from the very beginning or it will take you many months of mailing them postcards at a very expensive rate to become a brand in their hands.

On the subject of business cards versus digital cards, I've seen many people start trying to lead to the digital card. I do not believe that the digital card is the answer of the future. Handing out a business card is still a productive and knowledgeable thing to do. When you give somebody a business card, especially a business card that was made with quality and has great design features, it stands out.

People can physically hold on to it, and if they're truly interested in doing business with you, they will save it in their telephone. If you send somebody a digital card, they'll add it to their contacts on their phone, then forget who you are. That phone number will just fall into the other thousands of phone numbers that they have, and it will not create a memory in their mind for your brand. When I pass my business card to somebody, it has my logo on one side and my photo and my information on the other side.

For real estate, that's important. I want people to recognize my logo and remember my face. The more I hand out, the further that recognition goes. People look at it and say, "Oh, Kurz. I know who you guys are." If I were doing it with a digital card, no one would have the ability to look at my card, recognize my logo, and look at my photo to remember who I am.

TIP: Any way you can brand your logo and your business, do it. Don't find the easy way out. Brand yourself!

All of these things are important—posters, roll ups, and backdrops, and the ability to sponsor events so that your logo ends up in a slew of logos in a backdrop of a thousand photos to be taken that evening. Anywhere you go, ensure when you're promoting that you have backdrops and roll ups and posters to hand out.

It's imperative to consider these types of print items as well. So you see, print is far from dead!

Your logo is important. You must make it memorable, but please remember to make it simple enough to be embroidered and ironed on to T-shirts. Be able to stamp your logo on just about every single thing in the world. I make hats, T-shirts, yoga pants, and crop tops; I make tank tops, cups, water bottles, and pens. All of this is print media and marketing.

That is also something called **branding**. I want my pens in everyone's hands. I want my water bottles all over the gym. I wear a branded Kurz Real Estate T-shirt and hat to the gym every single day. As a matter of fact, I have my logo tattooed on my forearm so when I go to the gym, people joke with me. They come up to me and say, "Hey, brother, what company do you work for again? Ha, ha, ha."

Yes, we're joking, but guess what? You know my name and you know what I do; if you need me, I'm right here in the gym, every single morning, so let me know if you need anything at all. I'm also working out in the neighborhood my office is located in, so I'm sure you've passed by my office quite a few times and recognized the same logo prominently on the front corner. Your logo should be recognizable, it should stand out.

My particular logo is my name. I brand my name because I want people to recognize me as the owner of my company. That doesn't work in every industry, but it does in real estate, so I'm a big supporter of real estate agents promoting and branding themselves by their name and face.

I've tried other avenues, and I can tell you I've already failed down this path. When people talk about failing forward, I have done it three, four or a hundred times. I had different names for my teams until I realized that all the top agents in the world use their name. That's what they branded, so that's what I decided to do.

I realized that when I started saying, "Hi, I'm David Kurz with the Kurz Team," or now Kurz Real Estate, people were able to recognize me and say, "How are you doing? I follow you on social media. I have a cup of yours in my house. I use your pen all the time, it was excellent quality," so forth and so on. Branding yourself through print is important for your business. This is a piece of the foundation that will never go away.

No matter how digital the world becomes, you will never be able to drink out of a digital cup. Knowing that, why don't you make coffee cups showing your logo? These are called 'gift by design'. Hats, shirts, cups, and water bottles are imperative to your business. Why? The point of these 'gifts' is to give them away and spread your logo out.

We give away a ton of branded material because we want people to take our water bottles to the gym and on hiking trails. We want our name to be recognized by other people as they see the water bottle in someone's hands. We want to give them a ceramic coffee mug that will stay in a client's house as a consistent reminder. We provide them with a travel coffee mug that will be seen by them, their coworkers and their friends, when they take it on the road. Gifting by design is essential.

Recently we launched the website called KurzGear.com where people can purchase all of our Kurz gear and branded material. We found that so many people wanted our stuff that we couldn't sell it in-house fast enough, so we decided to create a web platform so that people can buy it at affordable prices, and just go about doing it at their own pace. On kurzgear.com, people can go there to purchase some of the things mentioned previously: hats, socks, cups, and balls, etc. We have them on there for people to buy.

Remember, when you're doing this, test this out. When I launched this store, I did it through different platforms. On those platforms, I made sure to order myself one of each item so I could check the quality. When I approved the quality, I launched the store to the public. I wanted to ensure that people were getting quality products even if they weren't directly from me, and that the third-party vendor that we hired to create these gifts, produced items at a high level of quality.

Quality is so important because it says a lot about how much you care about your business. Presenting the right material on print that you give away is important. Ensure that your logo is on every print item and that you've branded yourself accordingly. More importantly, ensure that your design does not stray away from the different pieces of material you put out there.

Your design must remain relatively equivalent or the same regardless of the many different prints and products you're putting it on so that people can recognize who you are and what you're doing and grow with you. This is the importance of print and the reason why print is not going anywhere anytime soon.

Bringing the Four Points Together and Creating the Foundation

Social media is free until you have to start paying to boost and create ads, so do as much as possible to promote organically on social media. Ensure your presence on social media 100,000 times a day (if you have to) to stay in as many faces as you can. Add everyone you meet on social media as soon as you meet them. Get them to follow you back. Promote your social media pages so people can follow you and want to see what you're doing.

TIP: Be interesting, but more importantly, be interested in what other folks are doing.

Don't just boast about yourself, but get in there and be interested in what other people are doing and commenting on their posts. Keep your comments intelligent. Don't be silly on social media or make yourself look juvenile. Get out there and be the person that you want to grow to be.

Your database should be growing on a daily basis. Every single person you meet should be going into your social media, into your email database, and you should be able to put all of this together. Your social media should feed your database. What do I mean? You should be connecting with every single person who likes your page on your social media. You should write them private messages, and ask, "Hey, would you like to be added to my email campaign?"

You then would send forms and requests for their information so that you can put this information into your email blast system software: Constant Contact, MailChimp, Contactually, etc. Grow your database on a daily basis using all the means at your disposal. If your friend's friend reaches out to you, they should get added. I don't care who you meet, your grandparents and their friends will go into it. Everyone needs to be involved in your database.

Your website should feed your database. I use forced registration to get people to sign into my website to request information, which allows me to turn around and send them emails from that moment onward. In my emails, I ask them to visit our social media pages and like them, so they become connected with me on social media.

People love to do that because everybody is on social media. Chances are that most people are on their social media sites multiple times a day, so they want to connect with you, especially if they're interested in what you're doing. Remember, be interesting, but also be interested. Get out there and connect with people, ensuring that your website is top-notch and a window to the world of who you are and what you do.

Your database knows about your website and your social media. Don't forget, every email needs to be connected with your social media and your website. You should have links on those emails letting people know how to connect with you. This is so important and it ensures that you have this perfect trifecta going on within your database- email campaigns, your social media and your website as your window to who you are.

TIP: Sounds like a lot right? Well besides hiring someone to do this, there are ways to automate these connections or personal touches. Look into creating emails in advance and look into programs that allow you to set up social media posts in advance.

Ensure that the three points are always connecting with each other.Last but not least, remember print items. Print always goes out to your database, from note cards to water bottles to everything in between. Make sure that as many people as possible have your logo and your business prints in their hands with a quality product. This is how all of this comes together.

We want to ensure that you take what you're reading today and implement it into your business, with the idea in mind that this will never stop. Every single day, you will be required to touch on all four points of this foundation and continue to build your business. I don't care if you turn your business from $100 to a billion dollars. YOU MUST TAKE ACTION. You've made it to the end of this book!! So don't waste this valuable time you've put in and do nothing with what you have learned. Put these things into action.

As the head of a multibillion-dollar company, you will still have to do all of this. The difference will be that maybe you're not the one doing it all. You will hire the right people at the right time to put out the right content and ensure that your business up continuously blows other companies out of the water.

Is this all that's required in business? Not quite, but these days, these four points can build a strong, solid foundation for you to become an influential entrepreneur. If you're looking to become an entrepreneur or you are an entrepreneur who currently owns a business, put these four points into effect and watch your business grow.

If you were to implement these four corners and build your foundation, no matter what you intended to do (as long as you're providing a quality product and delivering it in a quality way) you could grow your business with this foundation intact.

Don't ever leave mindset behind. Honestly, this is probably the hardest part of all of this: To have the mindset that will allow you to continue to be successful in your career. This is imperative and critical to your success. If you don't have the appropriate mindset to get the job done, then the foundation will not have a weak beginning.

Final Words

For my final words, I want to give you an idea. As an entrepreneur, I want you to understand that you will have to develop a very specific mindset. You will have to follow points in this book to help you grow your business to the point and level where you want to be.

I also want you to know that there are a million other books that can help you in your business. This book is about getting your foundation in order, other books will help you grow your business, and you should look into them as well. You should make an effort to read as much as you can, study as much as you can, and learn as much as you can to develop your business.

I speak to thousands of people constantly about developing and growing their businesses. I talk to thousands of individuals about putting themselves in the right mindset. However, I can tell you that very few of those people make an effort to do what needs to be done in order to create the business that they want to create. It's unfortunate, but it's the truth. People will go to a major conference with a major speaker and pay lots of money to listen to them speak, do a brain dump on their way to the car, and return to their life as it was before. Then wonder why nothing has changed.

Please, I beg you, don't be that person. Read this book. Come to one of my speeches, or listen to anyone's speech that will influence your life. Watch them on YouTube, watch me on YouTube and listen to what we have to say, because we're passionate about what we do. Our goal is to help you grow your business. All you have to do is TAKE ACTION.

TAKE ACTION in your life; TAKE ACTION in your business; TAKE ACTION in every single thing you do from your marriage, to your relationship with your kids, to the business that you do and your relationship with your clients; TAKE ACTION in your life today. Make a difference in what you want to do. Figure out what that is, lay out the plan and TAKE ACTION.

This foundation will be a great way for you to maintain your business consistently and grow this business. This is just a small part of it, but in my opinion the most important part, because without a foundation, you can get lost or broken easily.

Our next book will be entirely focused on the entrepreneur's mindset. I hope by the time you read it, you've already implemented a foundation in building and growing a solid business. That will help you settle in into your business with the proper mindset required to grow and become the superstar that you deserve to be.

If anyone is interested in contacting me, you're more than welcome to reach out at **David.Kurz@KurzRE.com**, or you can call my office at **786-529-5273**. If you're interested in working with me at our real estate company and you live in the local Miami area, please come out and visit me. I'd be happy to meet with you. To join Kurz Real Estate as an agent, you can email **JoinTheMovement@KurzRE.com** and one of our managers will reach out to you to set up an appointment.

If you're interested in hiring me for one of your speaking events and would love for me to come out and talk to you about everything that we've discussed in this book, reach out to me at **DavidAdamKurz.com** for more information. If you're interested in being coached by me, reach out to **DavidAdamKurz.com**, where you can learn more about my K Coaching program that is designed to help you in developing your business moving forward.

Thank you for taking the time to read this book. I hope that it makes a difference in your life- if it does, let me know. Shoot me a message, tell me how important it was, or simply tag me on **Facebook @DavidAdamKurz** and let me know that I've made a difference. My goal and my happiness comes from ensuring that everything that I do, whether it's writing a book, speaking in front of people or connecting with my agents, makes an impact. It means that their businesses grew or their lives changed in a positive direction. I want to know that your business has taken the next step forward and your life is changing for the better because of something that I may have said to you in this book. Have a fantastic life and ensure that you build yourself as an entrepreneur! And most importantly TAKE ACTION!!!!!!

73998635R00052

Made in the USA
Columbia, SC
25 July 2017